God of the Storm

N. G. Rudulph, Jr.

God of the Storm

Copyright © 2018 by N. G. Rudulph, Jr.

Library of Congress Control Number: 2018909891

ISBN 9781732437913

I dedicate this writing to my wife Vicki whose prayers and sacrifice have always sustained me.

Foreword

This is a heart book. Nat Rudulph searched his heart to find the words of truth and encouragement. Chaos and strife plague the soul from the sacred to the secular.

The question is "why is this happening to me." The answer is not easy because so much mystery surrounds the "why" question. Theologians, philosophers, educators, politicians, and celebrities try to calm the public square with answers that are tainted with ungodly perspectives.

Nat Rudulph uses the Word of God, godly wisdom, and real life experiences to offer comfort and hope during the hills and valleys of life. Each chapter resonates with real life. His answers to the questions of life are believable. He writes with compassion and truth embedded in each word.

This book is not an academic textbook and it is certainly not fluff and puff. It will challenge you to think seriously about God's nature and character. At the same time it shows the human race under the influence of sin. This book is marked with truth and sincerity. Read it. Muse it. Mediate on its content and find the blessing of God.

Martin Murphy
Author

INTRODUCTION

Jesus of Nazareth towers over history by His influence and His words. No one else has impacted humanity as He has. When one hears of His life from what is recorded in the Bible, there is no doubt of how profound are His teachings and amazing are His claims.

The way that Jesus presents Himself is not like a buffet where one can take what they like and leave the rest. The content of the Bible demands a choice, because Jesus confronts us with a choice: Receive it in its entirety, and so receive Him for what He claims to be, or receive only what you like, and reject what you judge unpalatable. But if He was all He claimed to be, you will be rejecting God.

If Jesus is who He claimed to be, then He certainly had (and has) the power to protect the historical record of Himself in such a way that it would be guarded from anything that would compromise the truth of the message.

My worldview, and therefore this writing, is based on the person of Jesus the Christ as the foundation and the Scripture as the framing of the building. Only the Scripture gives us the ultimate framework for life and true understanding. So only Scripture and other expressions which conform to Scripture can help us grapple with the very essential questions of tragedy and "storms" when they touch our lives.

I have deliberately minimized technical language. All fields of study use such language because it facilitates communication and clarity within the discipline. But it is often understood only by those in the particular field of study. For example, one could speak of the noetic effect, a theological term, which would leave many baffled, or one could say simply that humanity's mind is so affected by sin that they don't see things as they really are.

I want this writing to bring the reader to deeply appreciate the revelation God has given us of His incomparable omnipotence and grasp how truly amazing He is.

Table of Contents

1. When Bad Things Happen

Some years ago, Rebecca, the 21-year-old daughter of my pastor discovered that she had Lymphoma. She was the best friend of my daughter, Christine.

Through an oversight, the medical facility that had diagnosed her had failed to inform the family about her diagnosis at the appropriate time. As a result, she was unable to get treatment at an early stage, and the cancer became quite aggressive. By the time they found out, the prognosis was not good.

We were crushed and sought the Lord with all our heart. After much prayer, we felt encouraged and were convinced that God would heal her. She had treatment at one of the best cancer facilities in the country, but then, after a long battle, she passed away.

She was at home on her last day on this earth and seemed to have lapsed into a comatose state. Then, after a couple of hours, she became lucid for a short while as she lay upon her bed. She looked up with a gaze as if beholding something amazing and said, "He's so beautiful ...He's so beautiful!" Then she was gone.

The Sunday immediately after her passing, it became my responsibility to bring the morning message. I prayed, and nothing came. All I could think of were trite sayings we all have heard which I knew would neither comfort nor heal anyone's heart. Nothing inspired me; I was grieving as well. I had no idea what to say, but I was determined not to get up and repeat superficial platitudes.

Then finally I did something we should not do. In my grief and impudence, I desperately said to God, "Lord, I am going to open my Bible and if I do not get a word that makes sense, I am not going to get up there and speak empty words to these hurting people." I opened my Bible, put my finger down on a spot and the words were:

> The righteous perishes, and no man takes it to heart; merciful men are taken away, while no one considers that the righteous is taken away from evil. He shall enter into peace; they shall rest in their beds, each one walking in his uprightness. (Isaiah 57:1-2)

Another version (NLT) has it:

> The righteous pass away; the godly often die before their time. And no one seems to care or wonder why. No one seems to understand that God is protecting them from the evil to come. For the godly who die will rest in peace.

Every situation is different, so there are entirely different answers for others, but in her case, I knew the Lord mercifully shown me, in spite of my testing Him, that He had taken her home to be spared from some evil that was to come.

Sometimes God will help us find meaning in tragedy as clearly as this, but most of the time He will not. The temptation for us is always to wonder and speculate when something terrible like this happens, why it has happened. We wonder what they might have done to cause it, or if someone else did something to cause it.

The medical personnel who failed her could be blamed; a genetic defect passed down in her family could be blamed; the devil could be blamed; many reasons could be considered. But ultimately, regardless of intermediary causes, God allowed it, and He did it to bring about good, even though this was not at all apparent at the time. It took a revelation for me to get a glimpse into the "why," and to try and give comfort to the family and friends.

When a storm like this strikes in your life, the thought will come to you that this happened because you did not have enough faith. Or you didn't pray enough. "If you had just spent more time praying, it wouldn't have turned out like this."

Or perhaps you committed some sin, "If you just hadn't failed at that crucial time, this would not have happened." That is not the voice of God.

> There were present at that season some who told Him about the Galileans whose blood Pilate had mingled with their sacrifices. And Jesus answered and said to them, "Do you suppose that these Galileans were worse sinners than all other Galileans, because they suffered such things? I tell you, no; but unless you

repent you will all likewise perish. Or those eighteen on whom the tower in Siloam fell and killed them, do you think that they were worse sinners than all other men who dwelt in Jerusalem? I tell you, no; but unless you repent, you will all perish just like they did." (Luke 13:1-5)

The people around Jesus assumed that the people who suffered tragedy were being singled out for punishment because they were worse than those who did not suffer tragedy. Did Jesus say that they were worse sinners because this happened to them? No! He said, "...unless you repent, you will all perish just like they did."

God singles people out for mercy. It is the mercy of God which singles people out to not perish and to not get what all deserve. The explanation Jesus gave is that those who suffered tragedy were not worse sinners than the others. It is the due of all who transgress to be punished. What He was saying was that all of them deserved the tragedy that only the few suffered.

Another time Jesus healed a man who had been born blind. People asked Him if his sin or his parents' sin resulted in him being born blind. Jesus told them that it was neither but that the works of God should be revealed in him. In other words, even though it appeared to be a curse or affliction, in the final analysis, and from God's point of view it was not. It happened so God might be glorified and the man and his family be blessed. Blessed in a greater way than if the bad thing had never happened.

What can we see here? First, don't judge according to appearance (as Jesus said in another place). We do not see things as God does. The mind of humanity has been drastically affected by rebellion and sin so that our perception is distorted.

We tend to see humanity as having pretty good intentions on average, after balancing out all the people in the world. We look at ourselves and consider our good and bad characteristics and most people think the good outweighs the bad. From a human perspective that may be true for many, but we cannot see things from where God does. His perspective is very different.

> As it is written: "There is none righteous, no, not one; there is none who understands; There is none who seeks after God. They have all turned aside; They have together become unprofitable; There is none who does good, no, not one." (Romans 3:10-12)

This passage anticipates a question. The surprised hearer might ask, "You mean all? Surely there are some who truly seek God! Are you saying that not even one seeks God or does good?" So twice the writer emphasizes "No, not one."

The fact is, our nature is such that we are born separated from God and ready to express selfishness. A child doesn't have to be taught selfishness. Sin is nothing more than selfishness and particular sins are the manifestation of that selfishness. Sin is the nature or condition, and sins are the specific acts or expressions of that nature. We are fallen beings in a fallen world.

> But we are all like an unclean thing, and all our righteousnesses are like filthy rags; we all fade as a leaf, and our iniquities, like the wind, have taken us away. And there is no one who calls on Your name, who stirs himself up to take hold of You. (Isaiah 64:6-7)

Left to themselves, no one will seek God. We think of ourselves as born neutral – neither sinner nor saint, but then we get corrupted by the world – but the truth is, we were already corrupt inside. Our nature is corrupt, and that corruption is separation from God. It is not immediately manifested in a way that is ugly to us, so we think it is acceptable. But it is unacceptable to God.

2. Things Are Often Not As They Appear

A popular song from the 1970s by Paul Simon called "the Boxer" has the lines: "A man sees what he wants to see and disregards the rest." It is true that our motives and our separation from God color our interpretation of things, but our perspective does as well.

A few years ago I visited the rental house my parents and I lived in before I started school. I was about four years old, and in my memory, the apartment was large and spacious. I remembered that I liked to go into the kitchen with my mother and look out the window. I had to stand on a tall step stool to do this.

When I returned as an adult, it seemed more like going into a dollhouse. Everything was so small and tiny, the kitchen was minuscule, and the window was not high at all. We tend to see things according to our limited perspective.

Jesus told His disciples that He must go to the cross and die. After Jesus said this, Peter appeared to be giving loving advice when he said, "far be it from you, Lord." But Jesus recognized the source of this counsel immediately and said, "You get behind me, Satan!"

When Jesus was hanging on the cross, He seemed to be a failure. He seemed to be abandoned by God. He was rejected by His own people, and even His disciples abandoned Him. But this was not a failure; it was God's plan all along.

We see things inaccurately usually for two reasons: the attitude of our heart is distorted because of our own biases and sin, and our perspective is not objective. It is also impossible to be objective when what we are observing is incomplete.

Two revealing events in the Bible where things were "not as they appear" and not clear until they were complete are found in Matthew 14:22 and in Matthew 15:22.

> Immediately Jesus made His disciples get into the boat and go before Him to the other side, while He sent the multitudes away. And when He had sent the multitudes away, He went up on the mountain by Himself to pray. Now when evening came, He was alone there. But the boat was now in the middle of the sea, tossed by the waves, for the wind was contrary. Now in the fourth watch of the night Jesus went to them, walking on the sea. And when the disciples saw Him walking on the sea, they were troubled, saying, "It is a ghost!" And they cried out for fear. But immediately Jesus spoke to them, saying, "Be of good cheer! It is I; do not be afraid." And Peter answered Him and said, "Lord, if it is You, command me to come to You on the water." So He said, "Come." And when Peter had come down out of the boat, he walked on the water to go to Jesus. But when he saw that the wind was boisterous, he was afraid; and beginning to sink he cried out, saying, "Lord, save me!" And immediately Jesus stretched out

His hand and caught him, and said to him, "O you of little faith, why did you doubt?" (Matthew 14:22-31)

Behold, a woman of Canaan came from that region and cried out to Him, saying, "Have mercy on me, O Lord, Son of David! My daughter is severely demon-possessed." But He answered her not a word. And His disciples came and urged Him, saying, "Send her away, for she cries out after us." But He answered and said, "I was not sent except to the lost sheep of the house of Israel." Then she came and worshiped Him, saying, "Lord, help me!" But He answered and said, "It is not good to take the children's bread and throw it to the little dogs." And she said, "Yes, Lord, yet even the little dogs eat the crumbs which fall from their masters' table." Then Jesus answered and said to her, "O woman, great is your faith! Let it be to you as you desire." And her daughter was healed from that very hour. (Matthew 15:22-28)

As we compare these two events, we see a contrast between "great faith" and "little faith." Jesus said to Peter at the end of that experience, "Little is your faith." To the woman at the end of her experience, He said, "Great is your faith." These two parallel incidents seem entirely different at their midpoint compared to how they concluded. If only the first half of the narrative is known, one would assume that

Peter had great faith while the woman was the one with minimal faith.

When Jesus came to the disciples walking on the water, they were frightened at first. Then they realized it was the Lord, but none of the other disciples had the boldness to do what Peter did. From the perspective of that moment, Peter's actions seemed astounding.

Imagine yourself as a disciple in the boat. You would have seen Peter step out of the boat and begin to walk on the wind-driven water in astonishment! You might have thought, "Peter's faith is so great! I wish I could have faith like that!" The disciples must have admired him tremendously. Nevertheless, according to Jesus at the conclusion of the events, the faith which Peter had was actually "little."

One could argue that at least Peter had more faith than the other disciples. It seemed that way, but because it was little, it did not persevere in the face of the storm. When tested by something contradictory, it faltered and failed.

Compare that to the Canaanite woman. Jesus initially ignored her, so she went to the disciples and begged them. They were annoyed because they had just witnessed Jesus rejecting her. The disciples then asked Jesus to either do something for her or send her away. But he replied, "I was not sent except to the lost sheep of the house of Israel." In other words, I am not for her; she is a Gentile – I am sent to the Jews only.

Even after this, the Bible states that she came and worshiped him. Her response was "Lord help me."

If you were standing there and judged what was happening before the end, you might conclude that she must be a woman worthy of only rejection.

Still, she persisted in worshiping Him, humbling herself and imploring Him one more time. He responded by saying something that many would have considered an insulting slur. The Jews commonly referred to the Gentiles as "dogs." He said, "It is not good to take the children's bread and throw it to the little dogs." Some would have been offended at that – "How dare you call me a dog!"

Imagine the disciples' minds by now. They would be thinking, "What is wrong with this woman? She must be very stupid or a terrible sinner." Yet the same disciples believed that Peter had great faith when he stepped out of the boat.

Before the conclusion of these events, we don't know how things are, or how they will turn out. We don't accurately see into the heart of the matter, or into the heart of the people. It is unclear to whom God has given faith.

Even after this insult, she said, "Yes Lord, that's right, but even the little dogs eat the crumbs which fall from their master's table."

Had Jesus been trying to insult her? No, he was testing her faith. Then after she humbled herself in the face of apparent rejection, something remarkable happened. Jesus granted her request and told her that her faith was great. It is only recorded twice that Jesus told anyone they had great faith. Jesus knew she had great faith before this happened. He was not surprised and then suddenly changed His mind. He was not rebuffing her or being cruel; He was perfecting her faith – He was making manifest what was already inside of her and it proved her perseverance.

Often we go through storms, and we don't know why. Others, even our close friends or family may judge us like this woman was judged by the disciples. It may even seem that God is ignoring us; the heavens seem made of brass. Things like this happen so God might be glorified and we might grow into a deeper communion with God our Father and we will learn to trust Him more.

We never know how a thing will turn out until the end. Evil slaps us by surprise; then we discover God used it for our good. Apparent blessings turn out to be Trojan horses and not good at all. Then other times we never learn why things happen. It is not recorded that God ever told Job the reason for his troubles.

Everything we see and experience may often not mean what they initially seem to be. Jesus said, "Be wise as serpents, but harmless as doves."

3. What Do We "Know" That Isn't So?

Like warped mirrors in a carnival sideshow, there is a distortion in our perception so that we cannot clearly understand things. We see dimly, darkly, and in part.

Ronald Reagan once made a funny quip in talking about his political adversaries. He said, "Well, the trouble with our liberal friends is not that they are ignorant, but that they know so much that isn't so."

What do you know about yourself and about God that "isn't so"?

How do you think of God? Have you made Him over in your image? You may be amused at people whose idea of God is the caricature of an old bearded fellow up in the sky somewhere, and are certain you are much too sophisticated to think like that. But maybe you have your own image of God that "isn't so."

Our imagination can conceive of a being who is omnipotent, omnipresent, infinite, and transcendent. The human capacity for compassion, empathy, and love, can envisage a being who is perfect in the expression of these attributes.

But it is impossible that God could be directly known by our imagination or studied like a natural phenomenon. If this could be done, God would by definition be inferior to His creation. By the fact of being the transcendent Creator He must be hidden from what He created except as He chooses to reveal Himself.

God chose to manifest a primitive revelation of Himself in creation. This is seen in the design of all things, laws of nature, human behavior, our conscience, intuition, and imagination. But this limited knowledge is inadequate to directly know God. It convinces the human heart that such a being is possible and to the wise person, probable. But it does not lead to direct knowledge because it is partial and distorted.

People may grasp this but typically tend to think of God as a personal "errand boy" or "good-luck" charm whose main purpose is to benefit them. This is because of the selfishness and self-centeredness of our sin nature. Various cultures have gross perversions such as child sacrifice, but even this is based upon a corrupted view of the need to spiritually and legally make amends for transgressions.

Jesus presented Himself as the ultimate revelation and incarnation of God as well as the One who makes amends for all transgressions. He is the knowable expression of the unknowable; the bridge between God and man.

When I was a student at the University of South Florida in Tampa, I had a professor, Dr. James Silver, who ridiculed Christianity. He would even mock his relatives who were Christians, and derisively chuckle and say they were "praying for him." He was an agnostic and an existentialist. With him, there was no value or law outside of the internal person. He believed that we create our own nature and our own values through our free choices. He said, "It is the height of arrogance to believe that there is a God out there who is personally interested in you."

At the end of the course, I wrote him a letter in which I said, among other things, that the true height of arrogance was to presume to know that there could not be a God who could have the capacity to know about and care for every single person. I told him that he would have to know everything in the universe to know something like this definitively. To imply knowledge of that kind is far more arrogant, I said. It is arrogant because he was assuming his perception was exhaustive and comprehensive. He was, therefore, making his perception the final judge.

I also wrote him that even he would have to admit the quality of "personality" in an entity was more complex than "impersonality" and if that was the case, how could an impersonal God, a sort of "life force" create something more complex than itself. If we can create our own nature and own values, and they only have meaning to us, the very idea of values and meaning has to come from somewhere. If we can do that within ourselves and that is a subjective reality, how can we say there can be no objective reality? Can we know there is no God who could do that?

He wrote a letter back to me and told me about how he went fishing in the Gulf of Mexico, and a shark got a hold of some fish he had, and his net. He had a struggle with the shark and finally got away from it by beating it with a paddle. He then proceeded to tell me that in the big scope of things it didn't matter whether he beat the shark off or the shark ate him.

I had to shake my head at that. I wanted to respond, "If it didn't matter then why didn't you just let the shark eat you." An existentialist who follows the logical conclusions of his thinking will never carry it out in real life.

This same man, Dr. James Silver, told our class that he was an eyewitness to some of the events during a riot that took place on the campus of the University of Mississippi (Ole Miss) in 1962, while he was a professor there.

He was called into court to testify for the prosecution against a man he said was charged with using a liquid accelerant to start a fire. Silver said he rehearsed in his mind exactly what he had seen to great detail making sure he got it exactly right as a witness to the truth because he didn't want to make a mistake.

When he was on the stand, the defense attorney asked him to describe what he saw. He told the court that he saw the defendant go around the car and take the container out of the back seat of his vehicle. Immediately the attorney said, "Your honor, this man is a liar; the defendant's car is a sports car, and it has no back seat." Silver's entire testimony was thrown out.

He said he realized that in his zeal to make sure he told every detail in minute specificity, that he had unintentionally added some things that were inaccurate. He said that He was certain that the man got out of the driver's side and went around the front of his car to the passenger's side. He said he was also certain that he retrieved the can from the passenger side of the car. But as he thought back, he said, he realized that the man must have reached behind the front seat to get the can, and not into a back seat. Because it was dark and he was watching from the upper floor of an adjacent building, he said he obviously assumed something that was not clearly visible.

In my correspondence, I mentioned this incident as well and stated that even when we try our best to be a witness to the truth which we have seen, we are subject to defective conclusions because our knowledge and view is not exhaustive. I asked him how could he be so sure of things he could not see, when what he honestly did see ended in faulty testimony and resulted in a miscarriage of justice because his perspective and zeal had distorted his memory. Sincerity does not ensure accuracy.

When my daughter Christine was very young we were riding in the car at night, and there was a full moon. She kept staring up at it and finally said, "Daddy, why is the moon following us?"

Of course, I laughed a little and said, "Honey, the moon isn't following us." She said, "Daddy, I've been watching, and the moon goes everywhere we go."

I knew I could not explain to her the details of astronomy and how I knew that the moon wasn't following us, so I said, "It only looks like the moon is following us; really it's not. You'll just have to trust that your Daddy knows."

Similarly, our limitations cause us to misjudge many things. We overvalue what we think we know and a lot of it "isn't so" at all. We diminish God in our thinking by projecting our limitations upon Him.

The best example is the cross. Think about this fact: the worst thing the devil ever did was to kill the Son of God. It appeared at first as a tragedy, a terrible perversion of justice. From a human point of view, it was. However, that very same act was the greatest and most loving thing that God ever did – give His Son for us.

> For truly against Your holy Servant Jesus, whom You anointed, both Herod and Pontius Pilate, with the Gentiles and the people of Israel, were gathered together to do whatever Your hand and Your purpose determined before to be done. (Acts 4:27-28)

God was in control when Jesus went to the cross. He was not only in control; He determined the outcome ahead of time. He was accomplishing a higher purpose, not apparent to the observer at that time. The end purpose was to destroy evil and the devil's reign, and to redeem His people. We must get our comfort from trusting that God is in control and that He is in control for our good, and for the good of our loved ones.

Pastor Charles Stanley told about the time when he was going through a lot of difficulties. He was informed that people in the church were talking about him, and things were being said which were not true.

He told God he was angry at these people and didn't want to be their pastor and that if God wanted him to stay, He was going to have to show him how to cope with this. He said what God revealed to him was that He is sovereign, that He is always in control, and that He has a great fortress around him that nothing can penetrate. Stanley said he told God, "there's been a lot of penetrating going on lately it seems to me."

He said God assured him that the only way he could cope with these things is to understand that God was in control. He said he began to say "Lord, I receive this as from you, you are working something in my life."

He said he then found that he was able to forgive these people because they didn't know what they were doing. He said that he also began to experience the greatest peace he had ever experienced. And now, he said he understands that real peace and rest in God comes from knowing that God is always in control. Stanley said people will name some tragedy and say, "...but what about that."

He says that is not the question. The question is not something theoretical but it is day-to-day living. It is what comes into your life, not something you have observed in someone else or something that might happen tomorrow. You don't know all the whys and wherefores of the storm in the life of someone else. We are not qualified to pass judgment on them.

Going through trials is how we learn. Trials are like a workout at the gym. They are hard at first but produce endurance and greater strength. We don't accurately know ourselves, but God does. He lets us find out through testing, and he builds us up through it as well. Don't despair over it – let it be a learning lesson.

Concerning ourselves, we are like Peter. He didn't know himself when he wanted to walk on the water; he didn't know himself when he told the Lord, "I will not deny you." Then he denied the Lord three times.

Peter's faith failed initially, but he ended up being a pillar of the church, and there came a time when he did exhibit great faith after God finished refining him.

4. Is It Fair?

Some people ask, "Why do bad things happen to good people?" The better question might be, "Why do good things happen to bad people?"

Bad things happen to everyone in a world where rebellion and sin brought death and destruction and all the things that go with it. Good things happen because God delights in making exceptions and in showing mercy and grace.

People who appeal to "fairness" do not understand at all. It is "not fair," they say, when they hear of some tragedy. But it is fair. As hard as it is to say, all tragedies are the reaping of what mankind has sown; not necessarily what the person who has reaped has sown. That is especially what makes it seem "unfair." We are all in the same boat, we all suffer in the same household under Adam.

If your ancestors came to America years ago, someone else's choice determined where you would be born. You had no say in where you would grow up. Others made that choice for you. Adam, as the head over God's natural creation, made a choice. Like the captain who sunk the ship, every passenger went down with him.

Humanity is connected to Adam, just like the branches are connected to a tree. When Adam chose independence from God, which is sin, Adam took us with him. When the tree fell, we fell. We were born in rebellion and separated from communion with God. A tree that is cut down at the trunk still exhibits signs of life in the branches and may bloom for many days, but it is still certainly dying.

We all sinned against God in Adam; to put it another way we inherited the guilt of Adam's sin. This happened in the same sense as described in the book of Hebrews where it states that Levi (and also all his descendants) paid tithes to Melchizedek while he was in the loins of Abraham. Although Levi was not yet born, the action of his ancestor Abraham was attributed to him because he was in Abraham. "Even Levi, who receives tithes, paid tithes through Abraham, so to speak, for he was still in the loins of his father when Melchizedek met him" (Hebrews 7:9-10).

The same principle applies to humanity and Adam. The Word of God teaches "...through one man's offense judgment came to all men, resulting in condemnation" (Romans 5:18).

Some say they understand and agree that this is true for all of Adam's children, but their question is based on the fact that we are not only descendants of Adam, but as Christians, we are also of the second Adam, who is Christ. If it is true that we are in Christ (the "new Adam") and are new creatures, justified by God, and have Christ's righteousness imputed to us, why do bad things still happen to us?

While we do share a new nature with Christ and all other believers, we also still share the sinful nature with all of mankind, and that nature is called "the flesh." In Scripture "the flesh" means not only the physical body, i.e., the muscle, skin, bones, etc. but the entirety of the old nature. We also live in a fallen world where sin reigns and will continue to do so until the return of Christ and the resurrection.

Jesus said one cannot put new wine in old wineskins. New wine is a symbol of the Holy Spirit, while the old wineskin is a symbol of the flesh, or the old nature, which is dying and destined to disappear. Christians have two natures, but the Holy Spirit only manifests through the new nature.

The impartation of new life – a new nature – happens at regeneration, which is what being born again means. Jesus explained this doctrine to Nicodemus, "Jesus answered and said to him, 'Most assuredly, I say to you, unless one is born again, he cannot see the kingdom of God'" (John 3:3).

That new life has not yet been fully manifested, but is hidden from the world, much as the caterpillar has the nature of the butterfly hidden inside. The caterpillar appears outwardly to be just another worm, but it is far from just another ordinary worm.

The caterpillar cannot fly, so it is unaware that it will fly one day, but not as a caterpillar that has sprouted wings, or some kind of hybrid. It will "die" as to the caterpillar nature and fly as a new creature. The worm has "died" (undergone metamorphosis), and its butterfly nature will have been fully manifested.

In the same way, what appears now is not what the final appearance will be. Considering the heroes of the faith mentioned in the book of Hebrews, many did not receive deliverance in the "now."

These all died in faith, not having received the promises, but having seen them afar off were assured of them, embraced them and confessed that they were strangers and pilgrims on the earth. (Hebrews 11:13)

The object of their faith was never evident in their lifetime, but the proving of their faith was what pleased God. They confessed they were strangers so they would not lose heart because of the events happening on the earth or by the apparent and current measure of their lives in this world.

If we get a glimpse of what God is doing, it is apparent that His purpose is not to immediately give us all that He promised. However, we and the world around us are going through a time of proving and an outworking of His process of redemption.

It is a time of waiting and patience. The essence of what God wants from us is to stand fast in the midst of all that is around us defying us, denying us, and saying that we are a failure, or that God is a failure.

Have the attitude of the Canaanite woman of Matthew 15 who had great faith. The essence of faith is not doing great works like Peter seemed to have when he walked on water, but great faith always has these two elements:

1) Trust and endurance in the face of adversity.
2) The results are usually unapparent in the short term.

God is not finished with His people and He is not finished with the world. Though the wicked may prosper now, it is only that they may be destroyed later.

> O LORD, how great are Your works! Your thoughts are very deep. A senseless man does not know, nor does a fool understand this. When the wicked spring up like grass, and when all the workers of iniquity flourish, it is that they may be destroyed forever. (Psalm 92:5-7)

A senseless man, meaning the spiritually senseless, only looks at the outward appearance. People who question God as to why evil thrives and remains, and judge that it is not fair, do not realize what they are saying. The only reason they are alive is because He didn't already destroy the world of humanity when it was first deserved, but in His great mercy let their ancestors live and let the current generation be born into the world. So what they are really asking is, "God, why didn't you destroy us before we were born?"

God hates the sin, the evil, the destruction and awful tragedies that accompanied the fall of man and which dominate our world. He hates them more than we do. His heart is to destroy them. Since His heart is also to show mercy, He is temporarily putting up with evil. He let it fester and ripen, pile on up, and become more corrupt. He patiently waited for generations of people to come forth, over a very long time, so that He could save very many. God allows sin and tragedy to abound so that His grace and mercy may abound more.

> What if God, although willing to demonstrate His wrath and to make His power known, endured with much patience vessels of wrath prepared for destruction? And He did so to make known the riches of His glory upon vessels of mercy, which He prepared beforehand for glory. (Romans 9:22-23, NASB)

Sometimes we underestimate His grace and mercy and overvalue our own condition.

When I heard that Ted Bundy, the notorious serial killer, accepted the Lord a few days before he was to be executed in 1989, I was angry. I heard that he had prayed with James Dobson, asking for salvation. I did not rejoice that "a sinner repented," but was cynical and resentful. I hate to admit it, but my attitude was, "God, how dare you save this evil man! It's not fair!" I wouldn't say that to God, but He knows that is how I felt.

I had followed his horrific crime spree with disgust. He raped, cruelly tortured, and murdered at least 30, maybe 100 or more women, then abused their corpses. Attorney Polly Nelson, a member of his last defense team wrote: "Ted was the very definition of heartless evil."

However, as I contemplated it all I realized that I didn't accurately appreciate God's absolutely amazing grace, nor the depth of the sinfulness of us all. I did not correctly appraise the concept of "fairness," and I had a lot of unwarranted spiritual pride. I was like the elder brother in the parable of the prodigal son. The fact is, none of us deserve salvation any more than a man like Ted Bundy. It is not based on what we deserve. God does not grade on a curve, He grades on a cross. He substitutes the works of Christ at the mercy seat for those who believe.

Now, I have read things since then, which make me think Bundy was trying another con-game, so we don't know if his conversion was real. However, this experience revealed my heart to me and made me see how distorted our view of things can be.

A small law-breaker and a big law-breaker are both still law-breakers. They differ in quantity only. A glass of milk polluted with a tablespoon of sewage is not a whole lot more palatable than a glass of mostly sewage. I would refuse both.

I do not want "fairness" for that would mean justice equally applied across the board. I want the exception. I want His mercy and grace. Salvation and mercy are not about fairness. Fairness is an attribute of justice and the law. Mercy is not fair, it is an exception granting something good that is not deserved.

5. Three Things About Tragedy

God never promised us that we would be exempt from affliction. In looking at tragedy and suffering, we need to remember three things.

1. *The New Creation Life*

Many of the promises of God, especially those of a physical nature, are primarily for the new creation life. Therefore only a shadow of these promises are fulfilled in this current age of the old creation. They are not principally for this world, nor for these dying Adamic bodies.

When Lazarus was raised from the dead, he still had to die again, he did not receive the resurrection body – it was the revived and restored old body with the old dying nature which came from Adam. The promise of the new creation life had not yet been manifested, and it will not be until the Lord Jesus returns.

While God indeed heals and delivers in our day because it displays His mercy and He loves His children, He also has another purpose in this. It is to bear witness to the truth of the Gospel.

Supernatural miracles typically are sparse where the Gospel has already confronted the culture. Also, God "hides." In John 12:28-29 it states that the Father spoke from heaven to Jesus. But it also states some there who heard it said, "It thundered." Jesus prayed once and said, "I thank You, Father, Lord of heaven and earth, that You have hidden these things from the wise and prudent and have revealed them to babes." (Matthew 11:25)

All healing in this life is a temporary fix, a get-by, a shadow, a witness to the truth, a down payment on the new life to be fully manifested when the Sons of God are revealed as Paul talks about:

> For the anxious longing of the creation waits eagerly for the revealing of the sons of God. For the creation was subjected to futility, not willingly, but because of Him who subjected it, in hope that the creation itself also will be set free from its slavery to corruption into the freedom of the glory of the children of God. For we know that the whole creation groans and suffers the pains of childbirth together until now. And not only this, but also we ourselves, having the first fruits of the Spirit, even we ourselves groan within ourselves, waiting eagerly for our adoption as sons, the redemption of our body. (Romans 8:19-23, NASB)

He says we are eagerly awaiting our adoption – the redemption of our bodies, which will happen when God's children are revealed at His coming and He raises us from the dead, not before. God's kingdom will then reign in all created realms. So It is no surprise that in this context Paul continues:

And we know that God causes all things to work together for good to those who love God, to those who are called according to His purpose. For those whom He foreknew, He also predestined to become conformed to the image of His Son, so that He would be the firstborn among many brethren; and these whom He predestined, He also called; and these whom He called, He also justified; and these whom He justified, He also glorified. What then shall we say to these things? If God is for us, who is against us? (Romans 8:28-31,NASB)

Many people misquote verse 28 as "Everything works out for good..." but notice it says that they work for good to those who love God and are called according to His purpose.

His attribute of omnipotence causes all things to work out for good for Him. If we are called by Him and love Him, then by being joined to Him, He makes us partakers of what is true for Him.

2. *Christians Are in a Transition*

In this transition time, our purpose is to express mercy and comfort to all people and to be spiritual midwives to bring others into the kingdom and help them deal with the hardships of this life. We can identify with them and help them carry their burden.

... [God] who comforts us in all our affliction so that we will be able to comfort those who are in any affliction with the comfort with which we ourselves are comforted by God. (2 Corinthians 1:3-4, NASB)

As the kind of daily suffering Christ endured also takes place in us, ("...take up your cross and follow me.") We learn to console and comfort those around us. The message from the Apostle Paul is, "I now rejoice in my sufferings for you, and fill up in my flesh what is lacking in the afflictions of Christ, for the sake of His body, which is the church" (Colossians 1:24).

There is nothing "lacking" in the afflictions He suffered for the payment of sin and the redemption of His people. When Jesus said, "It is finished" His afflictions were complete. The term, "It is finished," in Koine Greek, and in Jesus' day was used to write a receipt for merchandise bought or work done, and it meant in that context, "paid in full."

So what does "...lacking in the afflictions of Christ," mean exactly? Notice Paul says, "...for the sake of His body ... the church." He is talking about the afflictions that we will endure that are a result of being sent into this dying, sinful world. It is sharing in Christ's identification with suffering humanity. He is still reaching out to and comforting people through us, His body, through which His life is expressed.

I heard once about a speaker who stayed overnight with a farmer and his family while he was in their small town speaking. The farmer had a sign in front of his house offering "puppies for sale." While the men were talking, a young boy came up and asked, "How much does it cost to buy one of the puppies?"

The farmer told him, "Fifty dollars, son. They are purebred and ought to sell for more, but I don't have papers on them."

The boy seemed disappointed at the price but asked if he could see them anyway. The farmer called the mama dog, and she came with four puppies. Then, a few seconds later, a smaller puppy came up, dragging one back leg.

The boy asked, "What's wrong with that puppy?"

The farmer said, "I took him to the vet, and he said that little dog doesn't have a hip joint and will never be normal."

The boy took a five dollar bill out of his pocket, and said, "Mister, I want to buy that puppy. I promise I will pay you five dollars a week until he is paid for, if you will let me."

The farmer said to him, "I don't think you understand, young man. That puppy will never be able to run or to play catch with you. He'll always be crippled. Why would you want a puppy like that?"

The boy just stared at the two men for a few seconds, then he pulled up one of his pant legs and showed them that he had an iron brace supporting a crippled leg. Then the boy said, "that puppy is going to have to have somebody who understands what he is going through to help him in this world!"

God has promised to be an ever-present help in our time of trouble. He came as a human being, He knows from personal experience what we go through, and He is going to help us in this world. We are also called to help others.

3. *God's Mercy and Love*

Since we know God, He has chosen us, and chosen to give us His mercy. We are valuable to Him, as valuable as the very life of His Son. And He is responsible for us – we are His family.

His love has no bound or end. He will withhold nothing to rescue His people and conform us to the image of His Son. If God is for us, who can be against us? His compassion exceeds anything we can fathom. Our love for others is a mere shadow of the astonishing love of God.

Consider how different God's wisdom is from the world's wisdom. In the world, it is the strong who inherit the earth. Jesus said it is the meek who will inherit the earth. God says the Gospel appears to be foolishness to those who are perishing. They think it is foolish, but it stands far and above any wisdom of man. The fact that they think it is foolish only proves that they are perishing.

God's love is far above our concept of love with no element of selfishness in it. God's ways are not our ways, and often we cannot understand them, nor are we entitled to an explanation. The bottom line is that we must trust God in every situation, and let Him comfort us because He has promised to do that.

6. Empathy Vs. Condescension

I recently saw a dog that had been run over in the road, obviously someone's beloved pet with a pretty collar. I felt sorrowful. Where do we think the empathy we feel at times like this comes from? Is God less compassionate than we are? Is He less troubled by this than we are? If we, being human, can be touched and concerned over something like this, how do we imagine that God is less compassionate? Our compassion originated in God. His eye is on the sparrow.

Empathy comes down and helps in compassion; condescension looks down and judges in self-righteousness.

At times when awful things occur, I hear people say, "God didn't do it, the devil did it," or the person "did it to themselves." These responses may be an explanation, but they are in fact superficial and cold.

If we did it to ourselves, or the devil did it, or if we are just the bystander reaping what someone else did, so what? Does knowing any of these things help?

After my pastor's daughter found out she had lymphoma he told me a couple in the church went to him and the wife of this couple told him she had a dream. The dream was about a shepherd who had neglected his sheep. She proceeded to tell him that she believed God was saying by the dream that his daughter had cancer because he had not watched his sheepfold and prayed as he should have and that he was a negligent shepherd. In addition, his son, who was not serving the Lord at that time, was in that condition for the same reason.

I've known of few things more cruel and more unChristlike. Even if the charges were true, Jesus wouldn't deal with it in that way.

People will tell you that if it does not go well for you, if you are not healed from a disease, or something awful happens, you are out of God's will or didn't have enough faith, because it is God's will for you to be on the mountaintop and walking in the abundant life all the time. They quote verses like: Isaiah 54:17 "No weapon formed against you shall prosper..." But they rarely quote verses that are equally about the believer such as: Psalm 119:67-68,71 "Before I was afflicted I went astray, but now I keep Your word. You are good, and do good; teach me Your statutes.... It is good for me that I have been afflicted, that I may learn Your statutes." Or as Paul taught "...we must through much tribulation enter into the kingdom of God" (in Acts 14:22, KJV).

Jesus said, "if they persecuted Me, they will persecute you." When Stephen was stoned, he looked up and saw Jesus in the heavens receiving him. Was he actually missing God's best? If you logically apply what some teach today, you would think he should have had more faith, rebuked the devil, and walked away from martyrdom.

Some were martyred for making the Bible available. Two were John Hus and William Tyndale. Hus was burned at the stake in 1415, and Tyndale in 1536. What was their crime? They translated the Bible into the native language that people could understand. Did they not make a sufficiently positive confession to overcome the enemy?

What about the believers being persecuted, jailed, tortured, and killed in our day because they profess Christ. Read Richard Wurmbrand's *Tortured for Christ* and then tell me it happened to him because he did not have more faith. This is what Scripture says about it, "For to you it has been granted on behalf of Christ, not only to believe in Him, but also to suffer for His sake" (Philippians 1:29).

Teaching people that it is their failure or lack of faith if they are afflicted, attacked, or not delivered from some tragedy is wrong on at least two counts.

First, it is simply not true. Believers are already delivered from the *punishment* for sin; they are in the process of being delivered from the *power* of sin. The promises of God concerning deliverance from the *presence* and results of sin such as affliction and death are mainly for the future.

If all the manifestations of the kingdom of God and the restorations promised were fully for this current age, then we would be able by faith to enter into sinless perfection. We would never be sick, nor suffer loss. We would also be able to "believe and confess" into our resurrection bodies right now, no need to wait for the return of Christ and His kingdom.

God makes exceptions in this current time of waiting before He returns and establishes His Kingdom. He intervenes in this dying world in the lives of His children. He has intervened in mine many times.

When my daughter Jessica was young, she and I were going in my car to a restaurant for breakfast one Saturday morning. As we approached an intersection, I noticed that the traffic light had just turned green, and even mentioned to her that we wouldn't have to wait for the light to change. Instead of driving on through, I put on the brakes and stopped at the green light. I sat there for a few seconds and then thought, "What am I doing? Why did I stop?" As I was about to accelerate, suddenly from the road in front of us came a loud hissing and squealing of brakes as a fully loaded log truck slid through the intersection with brakes locked. If I had gone on through the green light, we would have probably been killed.

The next evening at church was for a time of testimonies, so I stood up and told about what occurred the day before. I told them I didn't know if God had touched a "stupid" spot in my brain, or what happened that I would stop at a green light, but that God saved our lives.

Immediately after I spoke a lady that was there and seated behind us, Sonja Martin, stood up and said, "I was in the car behind you yesterday! God not only saved your lives but mine too! I didn't recognize you, and when you stopped at a green light I thought, 'what is this idiot doing?' Then I saw the log truck and thanked God that He had an idiot stop in front of me. I think we all would have been killed if you hadn't."

This is an example of God's providence. Of course, He could have prevented it in another way, a hidden way. He lets us see things like this from time to time, pulling away the veil, so to speak, in order that we might see His loving hands, even though His hands are there all the time.

This is why we should praise Him at inconveniences and when our plans are side-tracked. That person who cut you off in traffic might have been God's agent protecting you from evil down the road. "A man's heart plans his way, but the LORD directs his steps" (Proverbs 16:9).

One may say that inconveniences are one thing, but tragedies are another altogether. This is true, and I do not make light of suffering. But we are completely in God's providential control in every situation.

God's providence is often mysterious. God's providence does everything from feeding the birds of the air, to making His rain to fall on the just and the unjust, to protecting His children, and directing all of creation to fulfill His purposes.

Special providence is seen in events like what happened to us with the log truck. Supernatural miracles also fall under the category of special providence. What happened with the log truck, although it was extraordinary, and an intervention, could not accurately be called a miracle.

Most people think of miracles as physical signs and wonders, but regeneration itself is one of the greatest miracles. Think about what an extraordinary intervention it is to have a new nature imparted to someone! It is every bit a miracle as putting the nature of a walnut tree into a cactus and having it to bear walnuts instead of thorns. It is as much a miracle as when Jesus raised Lazarus from the dead. We start out spiritually dead just as Lazarus was physically dead. Then the living word of God comes to us, creates life, and we are born again.

Jesus was tempted three times to do miracles by the devil. Satan quoted Scripture to Him all three times. They were legitimate things the Lord would do at the right time, and were prophesied in the Old Testament concerning Him. But they were not what the Father had commanded at that particular time. He said He only acted on His Father's word, which was part of His answer to one of the temptations: "...Man shall not live by bread alone, but by every word that proceeds from the mouth of God" (Matthew 4:4).

The devil quoted the letter of Scripture to suit his purposes, but Jesus replied that we are to live by the word which proceeds from the mouth of God. The letter kills, but the Spirit gives life. The proceeding word is the word that is quickened or made alive by the Father.

It cannot be "confessed" into existence without originating in God and being ordained by Him. God gives faith by the impartation of His Word through His Spirit, by His initiation; it cannot be worked up or appropriated at a human whim. "Who can command and have it done, if the Lord has not ordained it" (Lamentations 3:37-38 NRSV)?

The second reason that teaching affliction comes from a lack of faith is wrong because it produces rotten fruit in peoples' lives. It indicates that they only have themselves to blame, or their lack of faith when bad things happen. They think that if God has provided all they need for victory and success, then they are the final determining factor. They vacillate between the euphoria of the mountaintop one day and the valley of despair the next. They fall into a kind of legalism, as well as condemnation, defeat, and self-obsession.

A self-obsessed person doesn't have to be thinking how great they are. It is also self-obsessed to have a pity party: "Oh, I'm no good; I am such a miserable failure. I have no faith." Either way, they are focused on themselves.

Someone came to me once and said, "I get so depressed when I think about myself." I wanted to say, "I get depressed when I think about you too."

The Almighty God is compassionate and faithful. He is a person, not a vending machine, where you deposit four quarters of faith, and then out pops a hundred dollar blessing. Faith and repentance are gifts from God; faith is not something we work up and then take to God for a reward. He is the Author and Finisher of our faith.

The ways of God defy our understanding. His grace and mercy are so much greater than we deserve, His mysteries are beyond our explanation and His purposes and power beyond anything we can imagine.

Ultimately, this life is passing away for all of us, but the life that is to come is the real thing. God Himself, the Scripture says, will wipe away all tears, and the storms of this life will not be remembered. Until then, we need to be comforted in this life.

7. God and Job

When Job suffered exceptionally, he asked God why. God did not answer Job's questions directly. He instead revealed to Job His greatness. The Bible describes Job in graphic terms. "There was a man in the land of Uz, whose name was Job, and that man was blameless, upright, fearing God, and turning away from evil" (Job 1:1). This Godly man constantly and consistently prayed for his family. But then God brought Job to Satan's attention. God asked Satan: "Have you considered My servant Job" (Job 1:8)? After that Satan began to attack Job, his property was destroyed, and then, all his children were killed.

Then Job arose, tore his robe, and shaved his head; and he fell to the ground and worshiped. And he said: "Naked I came from my mother's womb, And naked shall I return there. The LORD gave, and the LORD has taken away; Blessed be the name of the LORD." In all this Job did not sin nor charge God with wrong. (Job 1:20-22).

His three friends heard of it and came to comfort him. "So they sat down with him upon the ground seven days and seven nights, and none spoke a word unto him: for they saw that his grief was very great" (Job 2:13).

Job's friends had the good sense to be there with him after his tragedy without speaking a word for seven days. They expressed identification with him before speaking to his particular need. Their actions were saying, "I'm here for you; I feel your pain." They were right in this, even though their later advice was wrong.

Everyone offered counsel, and then Job questioned God. After everyone had spoken, God spoke to Job:

> Then the LORD answered Job from the whirlwind: "Who IS this that questions my wisdom with such ignorant words? Brace yourself, because I have some questions for you, and you must answer them. Where were you when I created the earth? Tell me, since you know so much. Do you know how its dimensions were determined and who did the surveying? What supports its foundations, and who laid its cornerstone as the morning stars sang together and all the angels shouted for joy? Who defined the boundaries of the sea as it burst from the womb, and as I clothed it with clouds and thick darkness? For I locked it behind barred gates, limiting its shores. I said, 'thus far and no farther will you come. Here your proud waves must stop!'" (Job 38:1-11, NLT)

Do you know the first thing about death? Do you have one clue regarding death's dark mysteries? And do you have any idea how large this universe is? Speak up now, if you have even the beginning of an answer. Where does the light come from, and where does the darkness go? Can you take it to its home? Do you know how to get there? But of course, you know all this! For you were born before it was all created, and you are so very experienced! Have you visited the treasuries of the snow? Have you seen where the hail is made and stored? I have reserved it for the time of trouble, for the day of battle and war. Where is the path to the origin of light? Where is the home of the east wind? Who created a channel for the torrents of rain? Who laid out the path for the lightning? Who makes the rain fall on barren land, in a desert where no one lives? Who sends the rain that satisfies the parched ground and makes the tender grass spring up? (Job 38: 17-27, NLT)

Do you know the laws of the universe and how God rules the earth? (Job 38:33)

Then the Lord asked Job a piercing question:

Then the LORD said to Job, "Do you still want to argue with the Almighty? You are God's critic, but do you have the answers?" Then Job replied to the LORD, "I am nothing – how could I ever find the answers? I will cover my mouth with my hand. I have said too much already. I have nothing more to say."

Then the LORD answered Job from the whirlwind: "Brace yourself like a man, because I have some questions for you, and you must answer them. Will you discredit my justice and condemn me just to prove you are right?" (Job 40:7-8, NLT)

I like the *Today's Message* paraphrase version here, it says, "I have some more questions for you, and I want straight answers. Do you presume to tell me what I'm doing wrong? Are you calling me evil so you can be good" (Job 40:7)?

This gets down to the real issue: man as his own god, deciding what is good and evil, and calling light darkness and darkness light. In truth, it is calling God up on the carpet to give an account as to why things are the way they are. This is evidence that we can't see things as they are. It shows the extent of how our arrogance and presumption clouds our hearts. Then Job replied to the LORD: "I know that you can do all things; no plan of yours can be thwarted. You asked, 'Who is this that obscures my counsel without knowledge'" (Job 42:1)?

God delivered Job and blessed him, but rather than explaining anything to him, He merely revealed His glory and majesty and power. The tremendous revelation of it humbled Job to the point where he had a better perspective of who he was and the vast chasm between the creature and the Creator.

After Job had prayed for his friends, the LORD made him prosperous again and gave him twice as much as he had before. All his brothers and sisters and everyone who had known him before came and ate with him in his house. They comforted and consoled him over all the trouble the LORD had brought upon him, and each one gave him a piece of silver and a gold ring. The LORD blessed the latter part of Job's life more than the first. (Job 42:10-11)

God asked questions that made Job realize that he could not understand a direct answer as to "why this has happened," any more than my daughter could understand what was going on with the moon.

God revealed his glory to Job because Job needed a new perspective. He had to be exposed to God's glory and greatness first, and humbled, and then he realized how presumptuous, unqualified, and uninformed he was to question God.

Most often the questioner is either not asking the right question, or is not ready to hear the answer. Keep that in mind when you are inclined to question God.

When the rich young ruler questioned Jesus, he was uninformed of his own condition, and not asking the right question. He came to Jesus and asked, "...what must I do to inherit eternal life?" Jesus answered by telling him to keep the Law, which was technically an answer, but not a real answer. For one thing, He told him to do something that no person with a sinful nature can do, which is to perfectly keep the law. All humans are born with sinful natures.

Nat Rudulph

The answer was literally the truth as to how one may inherit eternal life, but Jesus may as well have told him to sprout wings and fly, because no one can do it.

Proverbs says, "answer a fool according to his folly." Maybe that is what Jesus was doing. Why else would He tell him to do something impossible? Perhaps it was for the same reason God did not give Job a direct answer to his questions. He needed a new perspective before he could understand the question.

The Law requires a sacrifice that only God can provide. Jesus was not answering the question of the rich young ruler; He was administering the Law, to let it take its effect, as a schoolmaster, and get him to the place where he would realize his own impotence and cast himself upon the mercy of God. But as long as the young ruler thought there was something *he* could *do*, some performance, he was not asking the right question.

Jesus first asked the young ruler why he called Him good. He thought Jesus was just another "good" teacher who could guide him into more "goodness." Jesus knew the man did not understand the radical nature of human corruption, that "none are good," and there was nothing he could *do*, but was in need of God providing a sacrifice to inherit eternal life.

Likewise, God did not answer Job's question directly; he showed Him His glory and the greatness of His power.

> For my thoughts are not your thoughts, neither are your ways my ways, says the LORD. For as the

48

heavens are higher than the earth, so are my ways higher than your ways, and my thoughts than your thoughts. (Isaiah 55:8-9 NASB)

Some of the things we question require the kind of answers we are absolutely unequipped to receive. For example, how could I explain to my dog how my car works? I do enjoy his company, but there are considerable limitations to what could be communicated about the "how" and "why" of a vehicle. I am sure that my dog also enjoys riding with me, but there is no doubt he is content with letting the "mystery" of how the car works remain a "mystery." So we also should realize this is true with many things concerning God. Just enjoy "riding" with Him.

8. The Greatness of God

According to Matthew, when Jesus gave us the Lord's Prayer he ended it with: "Yours is the kingdom and the power and the glory forever. Amen" (Matthew 6:13, NASB). This was the paraphrasing of an Old Testament Scripture:

> Yours, O LORD, is the greatness, the power and the glory, the victory and the majesty; for all that is in heaven and in earth is Yours; Yours is the kingdom, O LORD, and You are exalted as head over all. (1 Chronicles 29:11)

Think about what this says:

> The power and the glory are Yours;
> The victory and the majesty are Yours;
> All that is in heaven and in earth is Yours;
> Yours is the kingdom, O LORD, And You are exalted as head over all.

In other words, all belongs to Him, He is exalted over all, and the nature of His power is such that He will have complete victory and glory in all realms.

> All the inhabitants of the earth are reputed as nothing;
> He does according to His will in the army of heaven

and among the inhabitants of the earth. No one can restrain His hand or say to Him, "What have You done" (Daniel 4:35)?

From the tiniest subatomic particle in the furthest reaches of the universe to the devil himself, God owns it all, and He has power over it all.

> [He] is the blessed and only Potentate, the King of kings and Lord of lords, who alone has immortality, dwelling in unapproachable light, whom no man has seen or can see, to whom be honor and everlasting power. Amen (1 Timothy 6:15-16).

Potentate is alternately translated as "the only sovereign" or "the only Almighty." It means that there is no one higher nor any power higher. He has no peer.

"Human defiance only enhances your glory, for you use it as a weapon" (Psalm 76:10, NLT). This is a fascinating Scripture because it shows that even opposition, or human defiance of God, is used by Him to accomplish His purposes.

As mentioned, the worst thing that the devil could do, was at the same time the most loving thing that God did – give His Son to die for us that we might have life. It was one and the same event. As Joseph said to his brothers who betrayed him, "You meant it for evil, but God meant it for good." As Augustine of Hippo wrote:

For the Almighty God, who ...has supreme power over all things, being Himself supremely good, would never permit the existence of anything evil among His works if He were not so omnipotent and so good that He can bring good even out of evil. (*Enchiridion, XI*, about 420AD)

But God does not react to the actions of man and turn things around. He is the prime mover. God planned to redeem man in this way, before time, before Lucifer was ever created and fell, and before man was created and fell. It was God's exact purpose to do this, and to do it in this particular way. Scripture calls Jesus the Lamb slain before the foundation of the world.

When the incomprehensible happens, and it seems that evil has prevailed, it is then that we begin to doubt. We wonder what is going on, but real faith persists in spite of what is seen and knows that God is in control. The highest expression of faith is in believing that He is in control in the midst of the storm.

This is why we are told: "Rejoice always....in everything give thanks; for this is God's will for you in Christ Jesus" (1 Thessalonians 5:16-18, NASB).

When things are going well, it is easy to give thanks. But we are called to thank Him in every situation. Regardless of how bitter something may be, if we obey this, and be thankful to Him, knowing He always has our best interest at heart, the

Holy Spirit will come in like a flood and comfort us in the midst of the storm.

Perhaps you are dealing with a storm, and the end is not in sight. You grasp what the Bible says about these things, but it seems like you are on a small island and you don't feel the mercy. I assure you that the embodiment of mercy is found in Jesus. Seek Him with all your heart. If you rest in Him, He will comfort you.

> I will bless the LORD at all times; His praise shall continually be in my mouth. My soul shall make its boast in the LORD; The humble shall hear of it and be glad. Oh, magnify the LORD with me, And let us exalt His name together. I sought the LORD, and He heard me, And delivered me from all my fears. (Psalm 34:1-4)

The Scripture says, "Magnify the Lord with me." Can we really "magnify" or make the Lord any greater? Of course not, but we can magnify Him in our own eyes and to the people around us. That's one of the main problems in the world and among Christians, we don't magnify Him enough. We diminish His greatness, but magnify ourselves, our accomplishments as well as our troubles, the world, and the devil.

We ought to pray: "Oh God, I magnify you – I lift your name on high! Your power is incomprehensible; You know the place of every atom in the universe; You know what is going to happen tomorrow; You ordain all things so that nothing can derail Your ultimate plan; You are so loving that you care about me more than my own mother; You number the hairs on my head; You even care about a sparrow falling to the ground. You are the ultimate artist and You reveal your glory in nature! Oh Lord, just let me get a greater glimpse of Your love and glory! Let me get to know You more!"

If we give thanks always for all things and in every situation and worship Him, we will enter into a place of peace; a peace that exceeds all our ability to understand. Understanding has limits.

When we experience storms our mind is always seeking understanding as a way to cope, because we think if we can find meaning at least we can begin to deal with it. But meaning only opens the door – the real comfort has to be personal. God came to us personally in Christ Jesus. He came to be with us, at our side, and in our lives with His presence in a real way. "... [H]e who loves Me will be loved by My Father, and I will love him and manifest Myself to him" (John 14:21).

Martha and Mary, sisters of Lazarus, sent a message to Jesus. The news was that "he whom you loved" (Lazarus) had become very sick. Jesus delayed going to see Lazarus, and by the time the Lord arrived Lazarus had not only died but had been in the grave for four days. The sisters, expressing their disappointment, both said at different times after Jesus arrived, "Lord, if You had been here, my brother would not have died." (See John 11:1-44.)

He could have explained that the Father had told Him to delay, or that He already knew Lazarus would be resurrected, or given them some other reason, but instead, He made no explanation, nor gave them any understanding. Rather, it says He was troubled and groaned in the spirit. He joined with them in their grief and wept.

> ... He groaned in the spirit and was troubled. And He said, "Where have you laid him?" They said to Him, "Lord, come and see." Jesus wept. Then the Jews said, "See how He loved him!" And some of them said, "Could not this Man, who opened the eyes of the blind, also have kept this man from dying?" (John 11:33-37)

We see two things here. We see the compassion of Jesus and how He identified with these hurting people in their grief. We also see how the mind of fallen man works in questioning the goodness of God and the power of God.

Timothy Paul Jones in his book *Christian History Made Easy* tells of how once in a class he elaborated profoundly (in his own estimation) about God's sovereignty, and how that God was always in total control. He then asked if there were any questions, and a woman asked, "If that's true, why did my daughter and son-in-law die last month in a car wreck? How could God let my grandchildren grow up without parents? How does God's sovereignty fit with that tragedy?"

He said his answer was empty because he spoke no words of comfort for her, even though it would have received high marks on a theological exam. He stated that he spoke the truth with "pristine logic," but he failed to "speak the truth in love" as Christians are exhorted to do in Ephesians 4:15.

The most important thing to do is what Jesus did. He came to be with us. When one is in the midst of the pain of recent loss, we need to simply remember to comfort them. They are usually not ready for explanations, and often even simple words are hurtful. Saying "I'm sorry for your loss" may feel empty and cold.

It is not the time to pat them on the back and say, "all things work together for good for those who love the Lord." A friend of mine who lost his son told me that upon hearing this quoted from a well-meaning person after his loss, he wanted to punch the person in the face and say, "how good is this punch working for you?"

We are so very valuable to God that He made an astounding sacrifice to rescue us from this fallen, dying existence. God embraced us to the point of becoming one of us. He was "manifest in the flesh" in the person of Jesus of Nazareth and identified with suffering humanity in the most profound equivalence. God the Son Himself took on not just sin and death, but our burdens and our miseries.

He not only suffered excruciating physical pain and a humiliating death upon the cross – as bad as that was – it was minor compared to the separation from His Father He experienced as a result of becoming sin for His people. When the Father looked at Jesus on the cross, He saw our sin and the punishment for it. Now when He looks at His people He sees the righteousness of Christ.

He took death into Himself. He is very God, all life, and all-powerful; He demolished death and its sting, proving it by His resurrection.

Therefore, when we grieve, we do not grieve as the world does; we grieve with hope, knowing that God is absolutely in control. But questions arise. Just how meticulous is His control? Does He really control *all* things?

9. All Things Are Your Servants

Forever, O LORD, Your word is settled in heaven. Your faithfulness continues throughout all generations; You established the earth, and it stands. They stand this day according to Your ordinances, for all things are Your servants. If Your law had not been my delight, then I would have perished in my affliction. (Psalm 119:89-92, NASB)

The Psalmist initially declares three things:

1. God's Word is settled in heaven.
2. God's faithfulness is throughout all generations.
3. God established the earth, and it stands.

Then he sums it up stating, "They stand according to your ordinances," or "according to what you have ordained" (Psalm 119:91). What is "they"? What stands?

Heaven,
Earth,
All generations,
His Word,
His faithfulness.

They stand according to what You have ordained, for "all things are Your servants."

The Hebrew word that is translated "ordinances" is more frequently used to describe a legal decision or a judgment, but the meaning depends on the context. The word ordinance is best here because the context describes God's ordaining of all things. Wouldn't heaven and earth include all things? Why does He add "generations"? The word "generations" means all families of man, all groups, all descendants, all history, all that has ever existed or ever will exist.

The Scripture here is emphasizing the extent to which the sovereign power of God reaches. Heaven and Earth include everything – the entire spiritual realm, and the entire natural realm. It is possible that the writer here adds "all generations" to clarify and emphasize that God doesn't only have control over natural matter and spiritual powers, both angels and demons, and over all events, but also over all people, as well as all nations and people groups.

He allows things to oppose His commands at times and at other times He intervenes and changes outcomes. God allowed David to sin with Bathsheba and to sin even more by having her husband slain in battle, but He intervened in the lives of Abraham and Sarah and prevented them from carrying out their deception involving Abimelech. He allowed Stephen to be stoned to death, but delivered Peter from prison.

> ...For I am God, and there is no other; I am God, and there is none like Me, Declaring the end from the

beginning, And from ancient times things that are not yet done, Saying, 'My counsel shall stand, And I will do all My pleasure,' Calling a bird of prey from the east, The man who executes My counsel, from a far country. Indeed I have spoken it; I will also bring it to pass. I have purposed it; I will also do it. (Isaiah 46:9-11)

Nothing happens anywhere or at any time apart from the will of God. However, if nothing happens on earth apart from His will, why did Jesus teach us to pray "Thy will be done on earth as it is in heaven"? How is His will done in heaven? In heaven, His will is always perfectly done. But on earth, His will is continuously resisted and opposed.

Since God's unstoppable power co-exists with rebellion, it results in the expression of two wills of God.

First, is His revealed will, which is also called His declared will, or commanded will. (Theologians use the term preceptive will of God for this.)

Secondly, there is His secret will, which is His decreed will – the Scriptural term is "His Counsel." (Theologians use the term decretive will.)

His commanded will is often disobeyed, opposed and thwarted, but His Counsel (His decreed will) can never be thwarted. This is what Psalm 119:91 means when it states, "all things are your servants." It does not say willing servants, or obedient servants, it says all things are your servants, i.e., all things do indeed serve you.

God causes His enemies to perform what He wills:

> And the ten horns which you saw on the beast, these will hate the harlot, make her desolate and naked, eat her flesh and burn her with fire. For God has put it into their hearts to fulfill His purpose, to be of one mind, and to give their kingdom to the beast, until the words of God are fulfilled. (Revelation 17:16-17)

It is also written that every knee shall bow, and every tongue shall confess, but it does not say how it will happen. It also states that all things will be reconciled to God, but it does not explain how.

Not all will be reconciled in salvation; some will be reconciled in judgment. Jesus said of Judas that it would have been better for that man if he had not been born, so the reconciliation of all, and the confession of every tongue, will not be a good thing for all.

All the unrepentant enemies of God, both angelic and human, will be forced to admit His greatness and His Lordship, by the sheer nature of His power.

He is the ALL-Mighty. He has ALL the might, and His power trumps all other power. It is this attribute of God's power that causes all things to serve Him.

"The LORD has established His throne in heaven, and His kingdom rules over all" (Psalm 103:19).

God's power is not defined as "the ability to do whatever He wants." That ignores His other attributes, and it ignores the nature of power.

There are some things that God cannot do because He is God. God cannot be tempted with evil. He is deserving of all glory; therefore, He cannot diminish His glory. Because He is the Almighty, He cannot fail to be in control of all things, since being less powerful than that would make Him less than omnipotent.

He cannot be limited by anything He created. Therefore He is not limited by time. If He were, then time itself would be greater than God. That cannot be. Everything that exists is either Creator or created, and neither time, nor faith, nor any other law, or "thing" is the Creator. He is subject to none of these.

A preacher once told me that God didn't know the future because that would violate man's free will. Although I had to laugh, it also occurred to me that at least he (unlike many others) had logically thought through to the conclusion of what perfect foreknowledge means. As Athanasius said (circa) 335 AD, "God did not decree anything because he foresaw it, but he foresaw it because he decreed it."

The Psalm continues to conclusion:

> They stand this day according to Your ordinances, for all things are Your servants. If Your law had not been my delight, then I would have perished in my

affliction. I will never forget Your precepts, for by them You have revived me. (Psalm 119:91-93, NASB)

This is how the Psalmist deals with affliction. He does not perish in affliction or tragedy because he delights in God's rule, God's Law, God's Word and God's power through which the Almighty decrees all things. "...He made a decree, which shall not pass away" (Psalm 148:6).

10. How Big Is Your God?

The critical question is "How big is your God?" Do you limit God? I do not ask if you limit what He can do for you. I do not mean how He providentially manages things or can intervene in your life.

Instead, this is not about you. It is about who He is – His nature and attributes. Do you limit Him by your conception of Him and make an idol out of your imagination of Him? Are all things possible with Him, or do you limit Him?

The Bible posits, "[He] works all things after the counsel of His will" (Ephesians 1:11). The Greek word for "works" in Ephesians 1:11 means His work is fully effective. In other words, He always succeeds in accomplishing His purpose.

"He works all things after the counsel of His will." What does this mean?

COUNSEL: the Greek word here is pronounced boo-lay' (βουλή). It is usually translated into four different English words: "purpose," "plan," "counsel," "will." From *The Discovery Bible Helps Word-studies* (edited by Drs. Gary Hill and Gleason Archer), βουλή means "a resolved plan, used particularly of the immutable aspect of God's plan – purposefully arranging all physical circumstances, which guarantees every scene of life works to His eternal purpose."

WILL: the Greek word here is pronounced thel'-ay-mah (θέλημα). It is translated into three different English words: "desire," "pleasure," "will." The revealed will of God reflects the desire of His heart. God desires that people obey Him and do righteousness, but He wills it in such a way that it can be refused: "Not everyone who says to me Lord, Lord, will enter into the kingdom of heaven, but he who does the will (θέλημα) of my Father in heaven" (Matthew 7:21).

It was not the commanded or revealed will of God that Judas and Herod and the crowds disobey God's Law by crucifying Jesus. But it was the decreed will of God, or His counsel (secret will), as confirmed by Acts 4:27. His counsel determined ahead of time that this would happen. The Bible states: "Him, being delivered by the determinate counsel (βουλή) and foreknowledge of God, you have taken, and by wicked hands have crucified and slain" (Acts 2:23).

"Determinate" means predestined. So it means "The predestined counsel of God," yet in the same sentence Luke says it was done by "wicked hands." It was sin, it was against God's commanded will, and was the work of Satan. At the same time, it was part of what God had ordained.

In this one act, He showed that both His love and His power are far beyond anything we can imagine. He did it this way to make all creatures, both those obedient and those rebellious, know that He is always, and infallibly, in complete control of everything, that His power is unthwartable, and He will always get all the glory.

His power is so great that He mocks evil by having ordained their very acts of disobedience to be the acts which fulfill His purposes. In allowing sin and rebellion against Himself to exist, His attributes causes the absolute worst expression of it to end up bringing about the very best of His purposes. The more evil their acts, the more He mocks them by His unthwartable power over them.

There can be no greater irony and consummate judgment than to have your enemies unknowingly, in their deviousness, willingly and happily perform the deed which brings them destruction, defeat, and torment, yet at the same time displays your love, goodness, and mercy. And it does so in a way that is delicious to the lost who have been found, and is so magnificently profound that the angels will sing about it forever.

God works through creatures who are rebellious and sinning through secondary causes, not directly, as God can never be the direct cause of evil. As Stephen Charnock, the English preacher who lived in the 1600s stated,

> God wills good by a positive decree, because He has decreed to effect it. He wills evil by a privative (depriving) decree, because He has decreed not to give that grace which would certainly prevent it. God does not will sin simply, for that would be to approve it, but He wills it to order that good which His wisdom will bring forth from it. He does not will sin for itself, but for the event.... To will sin as sin would be an

unanswerable blemish on God, but to will to allow it in order to bring good is the glory of his wisdom. (Stephen Charnock, *Existence and Attributes of God: A Discourse Upon the Holiness of God*)

Joseph's earthly father gave him a coat he didn't give the others, and his heavenly Father gave him a dream he didn't give the others. The coat made the brothers jealous, to the point they could not speak to him peaceably, but it was the dream that turned their jealousy into a desire to murder.

One thing about Joseph was that he was a trusting, naïve young man. He was without guile and pretensions. A vain man of selfish ambition would have never told his dreams.

Joseph probably expected his dream to be fulfilled right away; he probably had certain expectations of how it was going to be happen. When he had been sold into slavery by those brothers he saw in the dream bowing down, what do you think he thought about it? When he was framed and betrayed and sitting in prison, the Scripture says that the Word tested him.

It says, "He sent a man before them – Joseph – who was sold as a slave. They hurt his feet with fetters, He was laid in irons. Until the time that his word came to pass, The word of the LORD tested him." (Psalm 105:17-19)

Notice two things. The Scripture doesn't say the devil tested him, it says the Word tested him. It says God sent Joseph there before them, before his family.

This was exactly what Joseph said to his brothers when he faced them years later in Egypt and they were undoubtedly terrified at what he might do:

> Joseph said to them, "Do not be afraid, for am I in the place of God? But as for you, you meant evil against me; but God meant it for good, in order to bring it about as it is this day, to save many people alive. Now therefore, do not be afraid; I will provide for you and your little ones." And he comforted them and spoke kindly to them. (Genesis 50:19-21)

John Piper commenting on Joseph and his brothers:

> "You meant evil against me" (Genesis 50:20). Evil is a feminine singular noun. Then it says, "God meant it for good." The word "it" is a feminine singular suffix that can only agree with the antecedent feminine singular noun, "evil." And the verb "meant" is the same past tense in both cases. You meant evil against me in the past, as you were doing it. And God meant that very evil, not as evil, but as good in the past as you were doing it. And to make this perfectly clear, Psalm 105:17 says about Joseph's coming to Egypt, "[God] sent a man before them, Joseph, who was sold as a slave." God sent him. God did not find him there owing to evil choices, and then try to make something good come of it. Therefore this text stands as a kind of

paradigm for how to understand the evil will of man within the sovereign will of God. (*Suffering and the Sovereignty of God*, John Piper)

God Himself uses His enemies (and ours) to prepare a feast table for us in the valley of the shadow of death, in the presence of those who would destroy us, and would like to imagine that they could overthrow Him:

> Yea, though I walk through the valley of the shadow of death, I will fear no evil; for You are with me; Your rod and Your staff, they comfort me. You prepare a table before me in the presence of my enemies; You anoint my head with oil; my cup runs over. (Psalm 23:4-5)

God's enemies are still responsible and accountable for their evil deeds because it was the intent of their hearts to do evil. They act with the perception that they freely choose to make their choices. The fact that they are fulfilling what God ordained does not excuse them, nor does it make God complicit in their sin.

> But we speak the wisdom of God in a mystery, the hidden wisdom which God ordained before the ages for our glory, which none of the rulers of this age knew; for had they known, they would not have crucified the Lord of glory. (1 Corinthians 2:7-8)

70

This is the wisdom of God, which manipulated the devil, the ruler of this age. We can only stand in awe. "... [God] is able to do exceedingly abundantly above all that we ask or think" (Ephesians 3:20).

When Jesus prayed in the garden, He appealed to the Father to "let this cup pass" if possible, and then reminded the Father, "all things are possible with you."

He knew that He was the Lamb of God, pictured through the Old Testament sacrifices for generations; He knew that He came to die and told His disciples that He would be in the grave for three days. Perhaps He also knew that even if all that was so, and bound to happen, that because nothing was impossible with the Father, maybe the Father could still find a way to fulfill all that and yet somehow spare Him actually having to go to the cross.

Perhaps the thought crossed His mind about how the Father provided a substitute for Isaac and stayed Abraham's hand.

In the end, as He said at another time, He only did what His Father commanded, and so He prayed: "not my will, but Yours be done."

At the heart of what most people question about God and the storm is this: How could God be both all-powerful and all-good considering all that is in the world? It is a paradox and a mystery, but it is precisely what Scripture reveals about God and His creation. He is all-powerful and all-good.

11. Paradoxes and Perspectives

There are many paradoxes and mysteries in the revelation of God to us. It is human nature to think of God with limitations and attributes like our own. We must go by reason illuminated by revelation and not by reason alone.

Reason means the power of the mind to think, understand, and form rational conclusions through a logical process. Logic is inferring, or passing from one proposition, statement, or conclusion to another whose truth follows from it.

Revelation is God's supernatural communication of truth to the mind, and the Scripture is the ultimate revelation in a written form. Reason divorced from God's revelation will lead us astray every time.

Ultimately, the mystery of the kinds of things, which God has revealed cannot be fully explained – they must remain a mystery. However, a mystery does not mean that we take a blind leap in the dark, nor does it mean we must believe nonsense.

For example, Scripture states, "... the Word was with God, and the Word was God" (John 1:1). How can something be a particular thing, and yet be with that same thing? To be with something requires being different from it. To the natural mind that is nonsensical. But He both is God and with God. He is the expression of God or the Word of God, separate from the Father, yet He is also fully God.

God has given us parables, metaphors and other figures of speech; illustrations in nature, that enable us to communicate and touch upon some of these revelations in a better fashion.

Physical light has a dual nature, which seems contradictory; it exhibits properties of both a wave and of a particle, depending on how it is observed. Classical physics says it has to be one or the other. Some physics professors used to joke that on Tuesday, Thursday and Saturday they teach that it is a particle, and on Monday, Wednesday, and Friday they teach it is a wave.

So to explain this without the limitations of classical physics, Quantum Mechanics was developed to describe the behavior of small objects such as photons and subatomic particles. Quantum theory says a particle (for instance a light photon) can be in different places at the same time, like a wave.

Just as classical scientists wanted to say light was either a particle or a wave, the natural mind wants to make it an "either /or," to eliminate one or explain one away in terms of the other. If we can see in the natural realm such seemingly illogical and paradoxical things, how is it that we try to limit the revelation of God?

Scripture reveals the Father is fully God, the Son is fully God and the Holy Spirit is fully God. But there is only one God, one Being in three persons. No human analogy fully fits this. The Trinity is Unity in Diversity, the Other and the Self.

Another example: If you draw a triangle and next to it draw a circle, you could state that these two cannot be one object. One is not equal to the other. The triangle has three straight sides and three points. It includes definite beginning and ending points. The Circle has no beginning or ending point. It is continually curved with the same proportions – no points and no straight sides.

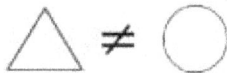

$$\triangle \neq \bigcirc$$

The characteristics which indicate that these are not equal are a description that uses the framework of two dimensions, Plane Geometry. In two dimensions they can never be the same object. To say that they are equal would be false in two dimensions. However, if we were to examine the framework of three dimensions, Solid Geometry, we would find a single three-dimensional object, which has the characteristics of both of these two-dimensional objects.

A cone contains in three dimensions what is impossible in two dimensions. From the standpoint of the top or bottom, the cone appears as a circle. From the standpoint of the side, it has the characteristics of a triangle.

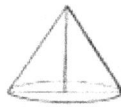

If there were a "flatland" where all things were only two-dimensional, then a "flatlander" would insist that he was looking at two different objects when he encountered the three dimensional object of the cone. In fact, it would appear as several objects, as many objects as he could find differing points of observation.

In the "flatland" world of two-dimensions, the two cannot be one. The natural man, the unregenerate man, is limited to a world like the Flatland.

> Now the natural man receives not the things of the Spirit of God: for they are foolishness unto him; and he cannot know them, because they are spiritually judged. (1 Corinthians 2:14-15)

The two-dimension/three-dimension idea applied to the triangle, circle, and cone, is a geometrical simile illustrating how what we might think at first are contradictions are only paradoxes.

Revelation is sometimes given to us from differing standpoints or perspectives. A good example:

> ... blindness in part has happened to Israel until the fullness of the Gentiles has come in. And so all Israel will be saved, as it is written: "The Deliverer will come out of Zion, And He will turn away ungodliness from Jacob; For this is My covenant with them, When I take away their sins." Concerning the gospel they are enemies for your sake, but concerning the election they are beloved for the sake of the fathers. For the gifts and the calling of God are irrevocable. (Romans 11:25-29)

Paul is putting forth two different perspectives or standpoints here: the standpoint of the gospel, and the standpoint of God's election. Paul is saying that the Jews are at once both enemies and beloved.

Israel rejected their Messiah and became enemies of God for our benefit, so that we, the Gentiles, might be saved. But he states that is true only from one standpoint, the perspective of the gospel, the good news to the whole world. He also states "...but from the standpoint of election, they are beloved for the sake of their fathers who were chosen."

The salient point to be noticed in this Scripture is that Paul is using the idea that there are two standpoints, or perspectives, in looking at one particular thing. He states two opposites, depending on the perspective.

What is a natural example? What about the sun? The sun is seen rising in the east; it travels over the earth, and sets in the west. We speak this way from our experience. By our observation, we conclude that the sun comes up at dawn, and goes down at dusk. It is obvious and self-evident.

If we observe from a solar or heavenly perspective, the sun is not moving around the earth, but the earth is seen rotating in relation to the sun. It causes the earth-dweller to see what appears to be a sunrise and a sunset.

With this new perspective, what seemed to be self-evident is not so evident. Considering different perspectives, we must ask, does the sun still rise and set, or does the earth only turn? This new knowledge of "earth-turning" does not mean the old idea of the sun rising and setting is "a lie." Both are true.

Even though the two facts appear as contradictions, it is understood that they are statements about observations that are both true but made from two different perspectives, or standpoints.

The sun still rises and sets, because we live in a place where we experience sunrise and sunset; our lives are centered around it. Just because we know that the sun is not really rising and setting from a solar perspective, that doesn't mean we say, "I'm going to wake up and go to bed at random times. I'm going to go to work, and shop at random times because the sun isn't really rising and setting."

That won't work, because every frame of reference as far as time and what humans do, is based on the sunrise and sunset. Poets write about it. Though they know the sun is not traveling through the sky, they do not now write "The glowing sky was bathed in the many glorious colors of an earth-turn." We still live our lives based on our experience on this plane.

Human responsibility is like the sunrise and sunset. The sovereignty of God is like the earth rotating in relation to the sun. The sovereignty of God and the responsibility of human beings are both true. They just appear to contradict.

Those insisting on a singular perspective ask, "If God ordains all things, why pray at all?" For one thing, we are commanded to. For another, it tempers our hearts and clarifies God's will to us. Also, we do actually participate in God's processes as the Holy Spirit prays through us, since from our place the future is malleable. This is a part of the mystery of how God uses means and secondary causes to accomplish His Counsel. He ordains both the ends and the means. God does not by-pass prayer and ordain things apart from the means of prayer when His will is to ordain it through prayer.

> ...we do not know what we should pray for as we ought, but the Spirit Himself makes intercession for us with groanings which cannot be uttered. Now He who searches the hearts knows what the mind of the Spirit is, because He makes intercession for the saints according to the will of God. (Romans 8:26-27)

This idea of differing perspectives is at the heart of many things in Scripture. This does not mean that you can force every concept into the idea of "all opposites are true from different perspectives." It only applies to absolute truth. It does not apply to error. Postmodern delusions are perversions, not paradoxes.

Postmodernism permeates our culture. An apt example of postmodern thinking was when a local minister here said to another minister in a public forum, "Do you believe that Jesus is the only way to God?" His answer was, "For me He is."

What if the question had been, "Do you believe that two plus two equals four?" and then the man had answered, "For me it does." Everyone there would have laughed out loud. It would be ludicrous because mathematical truth is universal. However, metaphysical truth is also universal.

Most people today actually accept his answer as sensible, because we live in a postmodern culture that has subjectivism and individualism as its guiding principles. It posits that there is no distinction between the truth and what one believes to be true. We live in a sea of competing "narratives" where nothing is solid. This is the spirit of postmodernity and underneath it is the idea of the "Absolute Autonomy of Man." This is not new – the ultimate idea of autonomy started in the Garden: "...your eyes shall be opened, and ye shall be as gods, knowing good and evil" (Genesis 3:5, KJV).

Personal autonomy appears to be self-evident, like the sunrise and sunset, to the unregenerated man. It is evident to him that he does what he wants, so he concludes he has autonomous free will; that he is what he wants to be, defines himself, acts independently of any constraints, and is not accountable to anyone.

> For you have trusted in your wickedness; you have said, "No one sees me;" your wisdom and your knowledge have warped you; and you have said in your heart, "I am, and there is no one else besides me." (Isaiah 47:10)

.

12. Can Man's Free Will Violate God's Free Will

When we grasp the greatness of God's power, and what Scripture declares on the matter, we see only God has true "free will," or autonomous will. Similarly, although we do not have autonomous free will, we do have self-evident freedom of choice along with the complete responsibility for all our choices and actions. The fact that we perceive a freedom to act makes us responsible. Charles Spurgeon said,

> That God predestines, and that man is responsible, are two things that few can see. They are believed to be inconsistent and contradictory; but they are not.... Two truths cannot be contradictory to each other. If then, I find taught in one place that everything is fore-ordained, that is true; and if I find in another place that man is responsible for all his actions, that is true; and it is my folly that leads me to imagine that two truths can ever contradict each other. (From the sermon, *Sovereign Grace and Man's Responsibility*, August 1, 1858, by C. H. Spurgeon at the Music Hall, Royal Surrey Gardens)

Unregenerate human logic typically leads people to conclude in favor of one side of this paradox and deny the other side. If everything is fore-ordained, they say, it means that fatalism is ultimately true; all creatures are robots with no responsibility, and God is the author of sin. They think that it doesn't matter what they do because "whatever will be, will be." However, it absolutely does matter what they do, and they will be accountable for every choice and every act. Or, they come down on the other side and say that God's power and will are limited by the free will of creatures. However, this is not found in the Bible. It is a philosophical observation that appears true to the mind of man, just as the sun's movement through the sky appears true. It can only lead to denying what the Bible does say about God's power, and it actually makes man in control of God. The Scripture nowhere says that God has limited His sovereignty in any way.

Man has free will. God has free will. God's will is more free and powerful than man's. God is not in any way limited by His creation, including man. God's power and freedom trump all other powers and freedoms.

People say, "God won't violate man's free will." They ought to say, "Man can't violate God's free will." God doesn't have to violate a person's choices because a violation requires a struggle. He co-opts the will of all creatures, all the time, and it requires no struggle or violation. The definition of all-powerful demands this.

God also co-opts what appears as "random chance" and the law of probability. To co-opt is defined as "to assume for one's own use; to appropriate." The disciples knew this, which is why they cast lots in faith as to who should be Judas's replacement when they could not come to an answer through prayer. "The lot is cast into the lap, But its every decision is from the LORD" (Proverbs 16:33).

Mankind is also co-opted by the devil as the devil chooses. Paul describes him in terms of "...the prince of the power of the air, the spirit who now works in the sons of disobedience..." (Ephesians 2:2).

Again Paul describes those who oppose God as ones taken captive by the devil, although they are freely choosing what they think they want.

> And a servant of the Lord must not quarrel but be gentle to all, able to teach, patient, in humility correcting those who are in opposition, if God perhaps will grant them repentance, so that they may know the truth, and that they may come to their senses and escape the snare of the devil, having been taken captive by him to do his will. (2 Timothy 2:24-26)

A rat in a maze freely chooses the path to the cheese, unaware that a scientist studying him has designed it to lead him to a particular choice. Bob Dylan once sang, "You're gonna have to serve somebody. Well, it may be the devil, or it may be the Lord, but you're gonna have to serve somebody." This is true.

God works everything after the counsel of His will, that's His perspective. It is the ultimate true perspective, which He has also revealed to us in a general way, but the particulars of it are usually hidden.

Joseph's brothers chose to sell Joseph into Egypt. They committed evil freely – nobody made them do it. They never considered themselves puppets in the hands of God. It was evident that they felt guilty and were worried about retribution.

Peter accused the crowd at Pentecost of crucifying the Lord of glory, yet went on to say it was done by the predetermined purpose of God. They were not excused because of that; in fact, it states that they were cut to the heart by what Peter said. They felt guilty because they were guilty and were responsible.

They acted with the conscious and real perception that they freely chose to make the choices they did. They were fulfilling what the devil wanted and manipulated them to do. They were also fulfilling what God had ordained to happen for His purposes. But, that did not excuse them, nor did it make God in any way complicit with sin or their acts, or the devil's acts.

People ask, "How can that be without them being turned into robots?" I, as a human being, could not do this kind of thing without making them robots. Nor could I do it without being culpable in their actions. But I, as a human, also cannot pay attention to more than one or two things at a time. God, however, can hear and focus on billions of people praying at one time, and simultaneously know the location of every falling sparrow, every hair on everyone's head and exactly where every sub-atomic particle in the universe will be all day tomorrow.

I can't fully imagine that but I can somewhat fathom that His knowledge has no limits. If His knowledge has no limits, why should we think His power is limited?

It is harder to imagine how His power works. If I can't imagine how something is done, does that mean I must reduce God into my size, with my limitations, when it comes to His power and His decreed will?

Just because I can't cause someone to serve my will without turning them into a robot, does that mean God can't? Is He limited like me? It is idolatry to presume that God has the same limitations as we do. The Psalmist explains. "You thought that I was altogether like you; But I will rebuke you, And set them in order before your eyes" (Psalm 50:21). The most precise and cogent description of this mystery I have ever seen is this:

> God from all eternity did, by the most wise and holy counsel of his own will, freely and unchangeably ordain whatsoever comes to pass; yet so as thereby neither is God the author of sin, nor is violence offered to the will of the creatures, nor is the liberty or contingency of second causes taken away, but rather established. (*The Westminster Confession, Chapter III*)

Consider the hardening of Pharaoh's heart. The Lord says to Moses, "Go in to Pharaoh and say, 'Thus says the LORD, Let my people go, that they may serve me'" (Exodus 8:1). In other words, God's command, that is, His declared will, was that Pharaoh let the Hebrews go. But from the start, He told Moses He willed to harden Pharaoh's heart so he would not let the Israelites go. This was His will of Counsel.

> And the Lord said to Moses, "When you go back to Egypt, see that you do all those wonders before Pharaoh which I have put in your hand. But I will harden his heart, so that he will not let the people go." (Exodus 4:21)

The writer of Proverbs has a similar message. "The king's heart is in the hand of the LORD, like the rivers of water; He turns it wherever He wishes" (Proverbs 21:1).

God's power and plans are above all that any creature can know. God does control all things, but He does not directly do evil. God accomplishes His good purposes through evil secondary causes. Jonathan Edwards said,

> It implies no contradiction to suppose that an act may be an evil act, and yet that it is a good thing that such an act should come to pass. . . As for instance, it might be an evil thing to crucify Christ, but yet it was a good thing that the crucifying of Christ came to pass. (*Works of Jonathan Edwards*, Volume Two, Chapter III)

Again from Edwards,

When a distinction is made between God's revealed will and his secret will, or his will of command and decree, "will" is certainly in that distinction taken in two senses. His will of decree, is not his will in the same sense as his will of command is. Therefore, it is no difficulty at all to suppose, that the one may be otherwise than the other: his will in both senses is his inclination. But when we say he wills virtue, or loves virtue, or the happiness of his creature; thereby is intended, that virtue, or the creature's happiness, absolutely and simply considered, is agreeable to the inclination of his nature. (Ibid.)

I like John Piper's insight on this, in which he was actually paraphrasing Edwards:

...[T]he infinite complexity of the divine mind is such that God has the capacity to look at the world through two lenses. He can look through a narrow lens or a wide-angle lens. When God looks at a painful or wicked event through his narrow lens, he sees the tragedy or the sin for what it is in itself and he is angered and grieved. But when God looks at a painful or wicked event through his wide-angle lens, he sees the tragedy or the sin in relation to everything leading up to it and everything flowing out from it. He sees it in all the connections and effects that form a pattern or mosaic stretching into eternity. This mosaic, with all its (good and evil) parts he does delight in. (*The Pleasures of God: Meditations on God's Delight in Being God* by John Piper)

You are responsible for what you know from your perspective. Regardless of God's hidden counsel, you are responsible for His commanded will. We urge people to repent and believe; we don't wait for God to call out His sheep without means. He uses means. They cannot repent and believe without being regenerated, and it is only through the message of Christ communicated through messengers that the Holy Spirit regenerates people.

For those who have heard the message of Christ there is a question. Have you believed? Not merely intellectual assent, but do you know in your inmost being that Jesus was put to death for your sins and that He rose from the dead? Do you know that you are forgiven? Do you know the Lord Jesus? If you know Him, you will know in your spirit that you are God's child. As Scripture states: "...you received the Spirit of adoption by whom we cry out, 'Abba, Father.' The Spirit Himself bears witness with our spirit that we are children of God" (Romans 8:15-16).

We are commanded to preach the Gospel to all, and the Gospel is offered to all. It is the kind intention of God toward mankind as a whole. It says "God so loved the world..." All are commanded to repent. All are offered salvation.

When a person believes and obeys God, it is God Who deserves all the credit and gets all the credit, as John the

Baptist said, "a man can have nothing unless it is given to him from heaven" (John 3:27). But if a person rejects God, it is all his own doing and he will receive the consequences.

Man's responsibility to repent and believe is like the sunrise and sunset. It is real because it is what we experience; it is where we live. The higher picture, the heavenly perspective, is that God's love and action towards us precedes our action towards Him.

"We love Him because He first loved us." (1 John 4:19).

13. God Uses Means to Fulfill His Counsel

As addressed earlier, God uses secondary causes, or "means" to accomplish His counsel. He generally does not ordain things independently of means.

A good example of how this works out in the particulars is in the shipwreck in Acts 27. Paul was on the storm-tossed ship, and they were all in fear of their lives.

> And now I urge you to take heart, for there will be no loss of life among you, but only of the ship. For there stood by me this night an angel of the God to whom I belong and whom I serve, saying, "Do not be afraid, Paul; you must be brought before Caesar; and indeed God has granted you all those who sail with you." Therefore take heart, men, for I believe God that it will be just as it was told me. (Acts 27:22-25)

Here was the prophetic word of God. What God spoke to Paul could not fail, or God's Word would have failed. The Lord prophesied, "God has granted you all those sailing with you." This was predestined to come to pass, as Paul affirmed, "I believe God that it will turn out exactly as I have been told." Then at verse 29, the sailors began to fear running aground and decided to try and escape. Verse 30 says:

But as the sailors were trying to escape from the ship and had let down the ship's boat into the sea, on the pretense of intending to lay out anchors from the bow, and Paul said to the centurion and to the soldiers, "Unless these men remain in the ship, you yourselves cannot be saved." (Acts 27:30-31)

Now if God had already promised to Paul all those with him, why was it necessary to warn them that unless they remained in the ship, they could not be saved? God told him he was giving him all of them and that he would lose none. Could the promise of God fail?

It was God's purpose to use that warning to keep the men in the ship and by that word fulfill what He had ordained. God uses temporal means to fulfill what He has ordained from eternity.

Similarly, the existence of warnings, which apparently are directed to believers does not prove that a regenerated child of God could be lost. It is like Paul's warning to these sailors, who he already knew were going to be saved, because God's word cannot fail. God uses warnings to keep his sheep in the right place. To be saved, they must heed His warnings, and they will do so because of His Grace. The truly regenerated ones will hear His voice and follow Him. He said, "All that the Father gives Me will come to Me, and the one who comes to Me I will by no means cast out." (John 6:37). He said, "of all those He has given Me I should lose nothing, but should raise it up at the last day." It is the tares who will fall away.

The warning in Hebrews states that it is "...impossible for those who were once enlightened... if they fall away, to renew them again to repentance..." but then it ends in a way that shows that those being described are not the truly regenerate.

"But, beloved, we are confident of better things concerning you, yes, things that accompany salvation, though we speak in this manner" (Hebrews 6:4-9). In other words, the falling away just described does not accompany TRUE salvation. Those who conclude that this passage proves a true believer could be lost, will also have to admit this passage understood in that way means those same people can never repent and be restored. In fact, many in the early church wrongly understood it to mean just that.

As the Apostle John said, "They went out from us, but they were not of us; for if they had been of us, they would have continued with us; but they went out that they might be made manifest, that none of them were of us" (1 John 2:19).

The warnings are like the view from which we see the sun rise and set – it is where we live. The promise of God is like the view from above, where the earth was turning, and the sun wasn't moving through Earth's sky.

Natural parables are by no means intended as an absolute answer to explain spiritual paradoxes or mysteries. They are a means to help grasp the truth, especially when it comes to the responsibility of man and the sovereignty of God.

Martin Luther had an unmatched perception of this matter. In *The Bondage of the Will*, published in 1525, he wrote a response to the theologian Erasmus of Rotterdam, who was making an argument for the autonomous free will of man and seemingly did not grasp the profound and paradoxical nature of God's will.

Luther designated the two wills of God as "God preached" and "God hidden." "God preached" refers to God's revealed will. "God hidden" is His Counsel. I have taken the liberty to edit a portion of Luther's writings noted in the next six paragraphs.

We speak in one way concerning the will of God preached, revealed, and offered unto us, and worshiped by us; and then in another way, concerning God himself not preached, not revealed, not offered unto us, yet worshiped by us. What we have to do with Him, is what is clothed in, and delivered to us by His Word.

God "preached" desires this: that, our sin and death being taken away, we might be saved; "He sent His word and healed them" (Psalm 107:20). But God "hidden in majesty" neither deplores, nor takes away death, but works life and death and all things: nor has He, in this character, defined Himself in His Word, but has reserved unto Himself, a free power over all.

Those not making a distinction between "God preached" and "God hidden" are deceived. The distinction must be made between the Word of God and God Himself. God does many things, which He does not make known unto us in His word: He also wills many things, which He does not in His word make known unto us that He wills. Thus, He does not "will the death of a sinner," that is, in His word; but He does will it by that inscrutable will.

It is rightly said, "if God does not desire our death, it is to be laid to the charge of our own will, if we perish." This is right, if you speak of God preached.

It is essentially necessary and wholesome for Christians to know: That God foreknows nothing by contingency, but that He foresees, purposes, and does all things according to His immutable, eternal, and infallible will.

Only God can do, and only God actually does (as the Psalmist sings) "whatever he wills in heaven and earth" (Psalm 135:6). The term "free-will" is a term that can be accurately applied only to Divine Majesty; for if "free-will" is ascribed to men, it is ascribed with no more accuracy than Deity itself would be – and no blasphemy could exceed that! We ought to refrain from using the term "free-will" when speaking of human ability, and let it apply to God only.

Believing in His sovereignty should help us to trust God and praise Him in all situations. It should also humble us before Him, and not lead us only to debate.

About 1400, Thomas à Kempis stated it well in the first chapter of *The Imitation of Christ*,

What good does it do to speak learnedly about the Trinity if, lacking humility, you displease the Trinity? Indeed it is not learning that makes a man holy and just, but a virtuous life makes him pleasing to God. I would rather feel contrition than know how to define it.... all is vanity, except to love God and serve him alone.

We should look to God and in obedience from the heart, "in everything give thanks."

Take the Bible seriously and ask God the Holy Spirit to give you a true perspective of true things. He is the Lord of the storm.

In the words of the poet William Cowper:

> God moves in a mysterious way
> His wonders to perform;
> He plants His footsteps in the sea
> And rides upon the storm.

About the Author

Nat Rudulph is a bi-vocational minister and a businessman. He owns a flooring store and a paint store in Selma, Alabama, and was ordained in 1994 by Liberty Fellowship. He has served as a Pastor and as the liaison for missionaries. He and his wife Vicki have done mission work in Latvia, and more recently in Nepal where they participated in a conference with about 300 Nepali ministers at a Christian school and orphanage in Kathmandu. The desire of his heart is to teach in such a way that the Holy Spirit will illuminate and apply the Word of God in clarity to every hearer. He has two bachelor degrees, one in Interdisciplinary Social Science from the University of South Florida, and another in Religious Education from Florida Beacon College. He has done masters level work at Regent University.